First published
Som Publishing
Birch Cottage
The Cross
King's Somborne
Stockbridge
Hampshire
SO20 6NY

Printer
Bookforce
The Olde Barns
Ailsworth
PE5 7AF
ISBN 0 9523827 4 1

DEEP FLOWED THE SOM

A childhood, a donkey and my Grandfather's whiskers

Words: Frank Cleverley
Drawings: Keith Chapman

SOM BOOKS

INTRODUCTION

Reflecting on a Hampshire childhood in the 1920's and 30's, this book of mostly verse recalls a time when travel was still difficult and rural areas so isolated that they seemed hardly to be affected by the outside world. To us, children of the time anyway, the village was our world.

This was the time of the great slump that had followed the industrial revolution. Farm workers were poorly paid and many were unemployed so that working class country people were poor, many of them so poor that they relied on the old Poor Law for subsistence. Workhouses too were full, in part because the tied cottage system in operation on most farms and estates meant that a lost job was also a lost home.

My Great Grandfather John Cleverley, who had lived most of his life and raised a family at King's Somborne, suffered the fate of dying in the Workhouse at Stockbridge, a harsh red brick building at the foot of Steepleton Hill.

That there was hardship then it is true, but since most working class people sharing these same circumstances, a strong community bond existed. Expectations also were lower making for greater contentment.

But the second world war that started in 1939 and the developments in communication that followed it brought to an end that comparatively innocent village way of life. Looking back on it now that it has vanished for ever, it was it seems, a magic time to have been a child.

INDEX TO THE POEMS

Title   Page

My Grandfather Fred Henley, my Mother's Father, was also
the father figure of my childhood, my Father having died
when I was still a baby so that I never knew him.

Born in 1859 in that same cottage we now shared with him,
Grandfather Fred was a widower from the time I knew him.
I was eleven years old when he died on March 13th 1932.
"Laid out" by the District Nurse in his newest nightshirt
he was the first dead person I ever saw.

A self employed Woodsman, he had worked the greater part of
his life in the woods around the village making the Hurdles
that were used mainly for sheep penning when Hampshire was
a major sheep rearing county.

Recording his simple way of life, the headstone on the
grave he now shares with his eldest son Leonard, reads:

1. Behind a black Gelding.

When he was born man could not fly
and God alone reigned in the sky,
the moon and stars supreme.

No tractors fumed upon the fields
to plough the margins, increase the yields
of oil seed rape and grain.

Great Shire horses, proud, majestic,
gentle, strong and non-pollutant
worked the land, and toiling,
moved at a sensible pace.
Not today's mad breakneck race.

Men carried messages, not bits of wire,
and those same men built the cathedral spires
in work finding freedom and dignity.
Now there is Social Security.

He never saw spacemen land on the moon,
saw Neighbours or Wogan
or heard Crosby croon.

But seventy years Hurdler and Woodsman, then,
to his last resting place he went,
quite rightly,
behind a black Gelding,
stepping lightly.

So home for me as a child was my Grandfather's thatched
cottage beside the stream that flowed through the Hampshire
village of King's Somborne, some ten miles south west of
the Cathedral city of Winchester and astride the old
pilgrims route, The Clarendon Way.

The cottage, in common with many others in the village was
poorly maintained and this is not surprising considering
the very low rents landlords were able to charge. Our rent
at the time was two shillings a week, that is to say just
ten pence in today's money. Compare that with your
present day mortgage if you have one!

Once one of a pair, the cottage had so deteriorated by the 1920's
that only the half we occupied was fit to live in.

But it was not all bad for it had a very large garden and an
idyllic position right beside the Ford in the stream where
steam locomotives crossed and stopped to take on water.
Something to interest boys was nearly always happening
there. It was alright for donkeys too, as you will see.

2. Home.

It was Grandfather's birthplace in 1859
and though by now it wasn't much,
there was a time when it was two.
But with the half not habitable
the donkey Jack made do.

It had never had a bathroom,
drains or running water, none,
except that is in through the roof
where it was far from waterproof
wide open to the sky above,
to let the rain come through.

A living room and a back-house
was all there was downstairs.
And the Privy in the garden
well, that really wasn't fun
as on a frosty winters night
in darkness but for candle light,
we shook with cold and fright.

Four shillings once a fortnight
the landlord called around
and said he'd soon repair the roof;
when Grandpa paid the rent.
And yes, of course, Grandfather said
he'd settle up the rent;
when the landlord fixed the roof.

So there you see catch twenty two
we couldn't circumvent it
and when the landlord
failed to press, we watched it
as it then regressed
and lived there through the years;
whilst it fell about our ears.

As a house it wasn't much
and now it's not at all
demolished by RDC
in time to save its fall.
But still we're sentimental,
it's quite natural that we are;
wouldn't you be? It was home!

With no plumbing, piped water or bathroom, water was drawn from a Well in the garden and hot water was heated in a large Copper in the back-house, a ground floor room with an earth floor that was used to store logs and coal for the living room fire along with bicycles, prams, gardening tools, food for the donkey, pig and hens and other sundry items. The living room fire was the only fire in the house so that bedrooms were icy cold in winter.

There being no drains, all used water had to be carried into the garden and poured into a large hole or trench where it soaked away naturally. In summer however bath and other soapy water was put to better use by being thrown over growing crops to kill aphids and other garden pests. It is an interesting sidelight on life 70 years later that, with metered water too expensive to waste, people have reverted to this most sensible and environmentally sound practice. Also the friendly practice of sharing the bath water has made a comeback. There's progress for you!

By tradition Friday night was bath night and then the copper in the back-house was stoked up, the tin bath taken down from its place on the wall and put down in front of the living room fire to howls of disapproval from boys who regarded bathing as a humiliating and unnecessary waste of time.

Strangely, I do not remember the copper ever being lit up for my Grandfather to take a bath, although I suppose he may have done so late at night after we were in bed. On the other hand perhaps he shared our views about bathing.

3. Bath Night.

In winter, when the north winds blow
and Sages forecast it will snow,
in the back-house, cold and chilled,
little washing is fulfilled,
by boys,
who hardly wash in summer.

Outside, stream water, petrified,
provides good sport to skate and slide,
grazed knees, bruised elbows, watering eyes,
fingers throbbing, as temperatures rise,
on boys,
who hardly wash at all.

When Friday evening comes around,
the tin bath's placed upon the ground
and filled with clear, bright clean water
drawn Crook and Bucket from the Well,
for boys,
who now must surely smell.

In the living room, oil lamp glares
and though the log fire roars and flares,
`pull the bath in closer mother',
cries my little baby brother,
for boys,
one hiding underneath the stairs.

Baby brother gets it first,
he kicks and screams, says it hurts,
Mum scrubs carbolic, up and down
he hollers, doesn't like the rubbing,
on boys,
one already blubbing.

13

And though the bath is near the heat
the door the north wind can't defeat.
`One side's warm and not the other'
grizzling, I complain to mother
for boys,
hot on one side, cold the other.

`Sit there in the chimney corner,
until you're dry and not a murmur'.
Jack's there now, and gets a ducking,
head pushed under, Mum's not looking,
at boys,
who split and tell on others.

And now at last three boys scrubbed clean,
but it won't last long, this cherub gleam
for Jack's already got his hand black,
punching me to get his own back,
and boys,
sent off to bed, no supper even!

Where it crosses the low lying Houghton water meadows the River Test divides into several channels and one of these, diverted to power the Horsebridge Mill, had a section upstream from the mill designated as "The bathe" where there were separate places for boys and girls to swim. The bridge carrying the old Southampton to Andover railway line divided the two, mixed bathing being strictly forbidden perhaps because most of us boys had no proper bathing wear and therefore swam in the nude or in our underpants.

The girls area was shallow and sunny but at the boys end, out of sight from the girls of course, there was a deep hole near a sluice gate where it was safe to dive without fear of hitting the bottom, but as the water was fast flowing and shaded by overhanging trees, it was cold, very cold, even on the hottest of days. For this reason many of us preferred the girls part of the river if we thought no adults were about. I'm afraid we often got caught.

With Mother's great friends our Aunt Dora and Flo Long we also went for picnics on the Downs that overlooked the river. The long walks to get there and those picnics remain amongst my happiest memories of childhood. Wild mushrooms that were as big as saucers and blackberries and hazel nuts were all gathered in abundance in season as Mother waited for the kettle to boil.

4. The Bathe.

In summer, when the weather is hotter
and we can swim the Test's clear waters,
with the tin bath we never bother.

Saturday morning, with towel and soap,
'rub it in your hair'. Some hope!
Follow the railway, walk the sleepers
though we may be caught or killed,
or even worse
need treatment from the District Nurse.

A Whistle sounds at Howe Park crossing,
wait and watch the goods train passing,
Fireman's thumbs up arm outstretched
as clanking, rattling trucks are fetched,
along the Spratt and Winkle line.

Stand on the bank as God intended,
is this bravery real, or is it pretended?
It's real for Sammy, for with one dash
he hits the Test with a mighty splash
and swims and dives, jumps in and out.
'Chuck my soap to me' he shouts
'come on in, it's really great'.

Shivering, cold, I start to walk
up to my hips and other parts.
My God! it takes your breath away.
And as I start to soap my head,
there's scum, to kill the brown trout dead!

Sam says `Let's go down and see the girls,
and I bags Beverley with the curls!'

With that he's gone, he's on his way.
And then he's there and in amongst them.
Some with knickers, some with none
they shout and scream and try to run.

`You grab Thelma, I got Beverley
Sam shouts, he's having fun
while I just stand there, shivering, blue funk,
and glad that Thelma has done a bunk.

And I get caught by Beverley's Mum
who boxes my ears, in fierce assault
whilst Sammy, near to the other side
scurrying up the bank to hide,
leaves me to scramble from the scene,
lost, one bar of Fairy Green!

The school established in King's Somborne by The Reverend Richard Dawes has a place in educational history, but of course I had no knowledge of that when I ran away from it at the age of five. Not that it would have mattered.

Right up until about the time this school opened in 1842 education in any real sense of the word was something enjoyed only by those able to afford home tuition or private or public school fees, but, despite the poverty he had observed locally, Dawes did not offer free places at his school. He believed that if people were asked to pay, however meagre the amount, they would appreciate it more.

He thought also that if everybody paid, then stigma that might attach to children of poor families attending without payment whilst better off families paid fees, would be avoided.

And it worked. With fees set at a low level even the very poorest of parents made sacrifices to send their children to the school. Places were soon in great demand and the school flourished, becoming a model for others up and down the land and a forerunner of education for all as we know it today.

5. Education.
(in honour of Dean Richard Dawes 1793 - 1867)

When God made the world, said he,
a place of order it must be
and He placed the fishes in the sea.

Some were large and some were small,
no equal size for one and all,
variety for God the call.

And when He saw that this was fair,
He made the birds, each kind a pair
and set them free to fly the air.

Thus happy so far with His hand,
He set the mammals on the land
and homo sapiens joined the band.

Some were strong and some were weak,
rich and poor, mighty, meek,
each his own estate to seek.

Some gained plenty, others not,
nothing equal in their lot,
but each in his appointed slot.

And though they quarrelled, fussed and fought,
each found a niche as God had thought,
poor serving rich, their labours bought.

Though poor men grumbled and complained
they were treated with disdain
and suffered hardship, hunger, pain.

For only rich men went to schools,
whilst ignorant workers stayed as fools
and only fit for labouring tools.

Thus down the ages, long we see
preserved this status quo shall be,
until in seventeen ninety-three;
came Richard Dawes.

6. School Days.

School is something that you love, or hate,
there is no in-between, no debate
and once started in an unhappy state
that feeling bad may not abate.

Starting school on my very first day,
not later than ten past nine, I'd say,
I'd had enough, no wish to stay
and didn't. I promptly ran away.

And though at the time I couldn't say why
school at first made me weep and cry,
I do know now what I couldn't abide;
it was all that **telling,** by those teachers on high.

Sit down, stand up, do this, do that,
come on out in front, put on the dunces hat.
Keep quiet, speak up. Oh! Do go away!
Run on out in the yard and play.

So I wonder still, are there those today
unhappy as I was, even at play?
Or have teachers learned at last, that they,
might ask you to do things?

Even at school!

7. Friday punishment.

Mu- u- um, do I have to go to school?
Grand-dad says he's never been.
`Well if you don't, you'll be a fool'.
Grand-dad then mum, is he a fool?
`Now boy, you know that isn't what I mean!'

Mu- u- um, Uncle Len then, he's no fool
and he never ever went to school
and now every day he's having fun
he's up in the woods and shoots his gun!
`Do go along boy, you'll have to run'.

Mu- u- um, what good is sums and jographry
if a woodsman I'm to be, and
Grand-dad says that he can teach me?
`Don't ask questions boy, you're late,
and teacher's waiting at the gate!

Go on, run along now, there's the bell,
pull your socks up, run like... pell mell!'
So now I run to meet my fate
and teacher waits beside the gate.
`What's your name lad, why are you late?'

You'd think he'd know it's me again
who only last week felt his cane.
He grabs my ear and pulls me round,
nearly lifts me off the ground.
There's that glint in his eye, anticipation.

`Friday, punishment!' Consternation!
Mu- u- um, do I have to go to school?
I don't mind if I'm a fool!

King's Somborne and the hamlets of Little and Up. Somborne lie along the course of the Som Bourne, the stream that gives the villages their name. I say along the course of the Som because that can always be found whereas the water has a long history of coming and going with the rise and fall of the water table.

King's Somborne was at one time part of the ancient demesne of the Crown and may have been important. It is certainly old, being in continuous occupation since about 600 AD and there being evidence of people using the site for more than a quarter of a million years.

The name with its pre-fix King's too is interesting. Doomsday, (1086), records that Edward the Confessor owned a house on the site that in recent times has become known as John O'Gaunt's palace, his wife Blanche inheriting it 1362. However, reproduction Doomsday maps give the name of the place as Sumburne with no King's pre-fix, so it is not clear when this first came into use.

Somborne seems to derive from Som or Sum, meaning swine or wild boar, and as a bourne is a stream, together they make "Swinebourne" or the watering place of the swine. And that is what it probably was. "Swinburna" too is documented.

The Church of SS Peter & Paul, dating from the thirteenth century and thought once to have been a Mother or Minster Church has been much altered and rebuilt. Brasses in the aisle that date to 1380 are said to be of John of Gaunt's Stewards, possibly father and son. Again, not confirmed.

8. Deep Flowed the Som.

How I wish that I had thought
to write about the Som
and how it looked in days long gone.
Of how it flowed from Crawley pond
through all the seasons,
on and on.

If I had only thought of it
when it was such a common sight,
to see it as its waters bright
ran over doorsteps, under doors,
flooding three feet deep,
and even more.

Of Geese and Ducks I could have told,
of Fodens crossing, Dennis trucks
and steaming Fowler Threshing Sets.
Of Moorhen, Coot, and Swan and Cygnet,
Sticklebacks and Todds and Redders,
Brown Trout up at Edderds.

And now though Mother Ussell's pond
is filled, and flat, and long since gone,
still there's a roadside ditch beyond
reminding those who saw and knew,
that Som once flowed there,
crystal clear.

In the 1920's and 30's village families were largely self sufficient in food. With large gardens and allotments they grew sufficient vegetables and fruit to feed the family through the year, storing for winter use all that was not consumed during the summer months.

Grandfather also kept a pig. It was bought at market as soon as it was weaned, fattened up during the summer and slaughtered in the Autumn when it was full grown. Then, early in the morning and accompanied by a great deal of squealing, its throat was cut and it was hung up by its hind legs in the garden to bleed into an old tin bath.

In the late afternoon when the bleeding had stopped and the carcass had been cut up there would be Pigs Trotters for dinner, Chitterlings for breakfast the next day and later, Black Pudding made from the blood. The head made Brawn and the bones, boiled with cabbage, made wonderful broth. Some of the pork was eaten as fresh meat, but much was salted down for later use, the most suitable joints being hung in the chimney to smoke into bacon and ham. Nothing was wasted.

And some things from childhood, those picnics, and the horrors and smells of pig killing day, never do go away!

9. Breakfast.

It's alright, I can eat it now,
the Army cured me, that I vow,
of my fastidiousness.
In the mess.

But she was so very small
when Grandpa bought her at the market stall,
a runt he said.
Stroked her head.

Smaller than Mouser the tabby cat,
with two small eyes, piercing black
and soft she was. A cuddlesome mite.
Clean and white.

In the back-house as one of us,
in a straw box, she lived at first
and we held her, stroked and stroked her.
Fed and fed her.

She grew and grew, got noisy, fatter.
`She smells' said Grandpa `we must move her
into the garden'. How she did cry.
In her Sty.

But she ate and ate the whole day through,
enormously fat and long she grew,
and also she got so very "high".
She filled her sty.

Then, coming home from school one day
and in the garden sent to play,
of Piggywig, no single sound.
Was there around.

`Where's she gone to Mum I pleaded'
and when at last my pleas were heeded,
`She's here!' Mum's finger up the Chimney, poking.
`She's smoking!'

It's alright, I can eat it now.

There are many pleasures in returning to old haunts, but it was with particular delight that I discovered on coming back to this village to live after an absence of fifty years, that the May tree that had acted as a corner post to our old garden fence was still surviving, although now in the garden of a large new house in place of our humble cottage of the 1920's.

10. Igg Agg.

After many years when, I saw her again,
the May Tree that stood in the garden.

Such a very dear friend, sharp her thorns to defend
the child's lost land of let's pretend.

Though the house is gone, she still lives on,
that Tree that as children we played upon.

First a sail boat, and then a plane,
the next day, back in the Crows Nest again.

But the thing I recall, the best of all,
is her ripe, red Igg Aggs, in the fall!

In the days before the National Health Service and Social Security, Friendly Societies had an important role in village life. At King's Somborne the most active of these was The Ancient Order of Foresters who, for a weekly subscription of a penny or so, provided financial help for members in times of sickness.

Every summer the local branch held a parade and a Fete in the meadow beside to our cottage and of all the regular village events, this fete was by far the the best, the most enjoyable and the one most eagerly awaited by the boys of the village. Not only for the parade and the event itself, but also for the excitement that came before it.

The arrival of J.Connelly and Sons great fairground steam engines with their gleaming brass roof supports, each engine pulling three or four wagons loaded up with all the paraphernalia of the fair, and then at the back the decorative living vans of the fairground families was the cause of great excitement, particularly for us boys.

A number of us waited at the top of Brook Hill from early morning for the first signs of arrival and then watched as sparks, smoke and steam filled the air as the engines make their several journeys up and down the steep hill to haul their wagons to the top one or two at a time.

One year there was more than the usual huffing and puffing to watch when an engine that had slipped off the road on the Mottisfont Straight had to be pulled out of the ditch by a second engine.

11. Foresters' Fete.

Each July, in the month quite late
when the Foresters held their annual fete
for the village it was such a great event
and everyone down to the meadow went.
Through the village a procession round
all lining up on the football ground
with at the front the Forester's banner
recruiting members at only a tanner.
And right behind that banner bright
came everybody's favourite sight
as Tommy Tott lead the Wallop Brass Band
the noise they made was really grand.
Brownies, Girl Guides, Cubs and Boy Scouts
joined by anybody else about
and Constable Taylor, a button shine beauty
down at the Green to do point duty
so many men, even some ladies bold
crowd the King's Arms, all the beer was sold.

Sun shining bright, what a marvellous day,
Colonel Bogey every inch of the way.

J.Connelly and Sons brought their travelling fair
Swinging boats, Boxing Booth and Hoopla there
three darts for tuppence, pierce three cards
to win you a bubble pipe, made of shards.
At the boxing booth, Joe Beckett's brother
throws out a challenge to one and the other.
When one brave villager took to the ring
enduring a three rounds battering
his courageous challenge he had downed
all for a dollar, or two half crowns.
In the swinging boats two village clowns
soared so high that the attendant frowned
put on the drag bar, brought them down.
Coco-nuts glued to the cups we hit
roll your penny, but the squares wouldn't fit
try your strength, can you ring the bell?
Let Gypsy Rose Lee your fortune tell.

Galloping Horses, steam organ swaying
God save the King, already playing?

November 11th, Armistice Day, was quite a different day.

A service of thanksgiving and remembrance was held around the new war memorial or in the church with a Bugler to blow the Last Post and I suppose I felt more involved than most because my Father had died as a result of the war.

Nearly all the school, non-conformists not being obliged to take part, went in procession from the school and when I sang in the Choir for the first time at the age of eight and the 1914-18 war was still fresh in the memory, many in the congregation, including some of the men, wept openly at the sound of the bugle. One man I learned later had lost both his brothers to the war, one of them on the very last day of fighting. Who wouldn't weep for such cruel tragedy?

The War memorial, erected in 1921, was presented to the village by Herbert Johnson, a stockbroker and the last true Lord of the Ashley Manor. It is one of only a very few "listed building" village war memorials, having been designed by Sir Edwin Lutyens who also designed Herbert Johnson's huge brick and chalk mansion at Marshcourt.

12. Armistice.

On Armistice day we remembered the dead
of Verdun, Somme, Arras, Mons,
Gallipoli, Ypres, Vimy, Marne,
and we wore the poppies of Flanders field.

We mourned shattered bodies, blinded eyes,
the blood, the tears, the terrifying fears
of men that died, of the mothers that cried
and the widowed wives, with empty lives.

This was the war that would end all war,
we'd never have to fight again,
yet still we hear that age old call,
`Your country needs you, one and all'.

So was it all just hypocrisy
the prayers and tears upon this day?
And is there not to be a better way
than `send a task force, and make them pay?'

For surely man can see today
that the price of war is just too high?
And that there has to be and end to it
now there is nowhere left to hide!

13. The Woodsman.

As in Humbers Wood, I lie
with lazy glance to watch the sky
through hazel branches reaching high
to see white clouds, go drifting by.

And see The Woodsman take his stone
with swishing strokes, his axe to hone,
steely bright the edge producing,
razor like, sharp, hair splitting.

Then tree by tree he strikes the stumps,
they shake and quiver, softly falls
the shower of green leaves, unripe fruit
and sunlight shafts in swift pursuit.

Rhythmic chopping, tree on tree
muttered curses in between,
`Damn that knot and curse the scree.
Boy, pull this bramble off my knee!'

And ever wider grows the sky
with darker, grey clouds now on high.
`Needs must hurry boy, 'twill rain
before the sun is up again.'

Then as the last tree shudders, 'lights,
high in the canopy and sitting tight,
Squirrel, twitching tail in sight
jumps, quantum leap, flees, startled, fright.

The Woodsman, wholly unaware,
now hones his hook the rods to pare
and deftly splits them, that way, this
still soft with sap, they bend and twist.

Gnarled, horny hands and eagle eye,
selects and grades them, puts them by.

'Neath lowering skies then homeward we,
`When Humbers next we cut', says he,
`you'll be grown man, as tall as me,
and a double harvest there will be'.

`Come boy, don't dream', he calls, ahead,
waits, takes my hand and footsteps sped.
`Come boy, don't dawdle, keep with me,
I smell already our rabbit for tea'...

...as dreaming dreams I fall behind,
with full grown hazel on my mind
and thoughts of axe head's flashing whine.
But dreams are idle; his; and mine.

For he cannot know, and still less me
that before that canopy again grows free,
gnarled horny hand, now warm in mine,
long cold, and long, long dead will be.

And now the hazel, tall and straight
stands ready, needs be that it must wait
for deep beneath his tombstone he,
Fred Henley. Woodsman. Seventy-three.

Gone, dead too, fond dreams of childhood
flying axehead, falling wood,
for though full grown and tall as he,
I follow some lesser destiny.

But wait now! Surely that's a ghost I see?
and that the smell of rabbit tea?
As watching in Humbers now I see,
Squirrel, still fly the canopy!

14. The dreamless dream.

Asleep,
beneath the burnished elm
the screws of brass,
he dreams,
as he dreamed in his Donkey Cart.
Clip clop. clip clop.

       The strap,
         broad band of leather
       buckle of brass
    adorns the bedroom chair,
  he dreams,
down, down, the narrow stair.

     Shining hearse
     Gelding black,
     head feathers dancing...
     ...bright medals of brass,
     he dreams,
     that he's still in his Donkey Cart.

    Clip clop. Clip, clop.

Donkey Jack
in the meadow grazing,
lifts his head, hesitates
resumes the grazing,
dreams not,
that it's his master; passing.

Here, there
a curtsy dropped,
bare head bowed low, a downcast eye,
sombre the knell, intoning bell,
he dreams,
of the dreams that passed him by.

Black, black,
the cassock that waits
and footsteps that echo upon the aisle,
footsteps that echo, fade away,
he dreams,
as he dreamed on his christening day.

Ashes to ashes,
dust to dust
rattle upon the coffin lid
the plate of brass, but wake him not,
he dreams,
the dreamless dream, at last.

Clip clop, clip, clop; clip; clop.

Between the wars, at least until re-armament created more work in about 1937, many villagers were forced to fall back on Parish Poor Relief. The Poor Law Officer was a frequent visitor to the village and when, with my Grandfather's death the family lost the breadwinner, he came in his motor car to see my Mother, probably at the request of the Vicar

Looking affluent in his country tweeds, he stood in the living room surveying Grandfather's precious possessions and picked out a small and very old oak swivel action round table my Grandfather had treasured. `You can get a good price for that table dear lady, you'll have to sell it before I can help you I'm afraid. I can send a man round if you wish me to' he said.

Later my Mother was later paid ten shillings for the table together with several other items, the real value being ten times that at least. It was no wonder that Dawes had said he found villagers `demoralized by the old poor law' if that is how it worked! Those more accustomed to these visits said that they hid anything of value before the poor law man arrived.

Things only began to look up when my brother John left school in 1933 and boosted the family budget by about seven shillings and six pence a week. The corner was turned and from then on things were on the up and up, but not before my Mother had very nearly died in Winchester Hospital of pneumonia and bronchitis brought on by exhaustion and malnutrition. Then the war came!

15. Parish poor relief.

Grandfather Fred, is dead.
Where shall we get bread?
Who will protect us, and keep us,
now that he's left us?

And when the knell, that intoning bell
ceases to sound, who'll be around?
Take in washing, scrub peoples floors,
anything other than begging at doors.

Three babies to feed, provide for their need,
is there no-one this desperate plight to heed?
What of the Vicar? Perhaps he may knock
for he stands in the pulpit, calls us his flock.

And now he is here, but not with much cheer.
`There are too many poor, sorry my dear!
There's not enough money, can't make it go round,
perhaps in the Workhouse a place can be found'.

The Poor Law man, then he comes to see,
`Chattles must go, that's the rule' says he
and he sends round a dealer, a crony no doubt
who leaves table, chairs, beds. Carts the rest out.

He pays us a pittance, he makes a pile,
but there's food on the table.
At least for a while.

16. Twelve.

When I was twelve in thirty three,
and Barbara sat in the desk behind me,
giving me a come-on look
she winked her eye and smiled at me,
as though she would my sweetheart be.

Our initials I drew, all intertwined
and underscored with "please be mine",
then with my hand behind me reaching
I held it out, whilst at the same time
making out to heed the teaching.

I felt no soft hand touching mine,
no longed for fingers were combined
and thinking that she hadn't seen,
I gently shook my hand about.
Alas, alack, the note fell out.

And Mrs Matthew shuts her book,
glares at us with a withering look.

`I'll never speak to you again'
Barbara says, and brings me pain.
Heart that's aching, heavy, breaking,
I'll never love again, it's too grief making.

`Are you coming for a walk Frank
up to the Rec, or to the Green Bank?
Heart that's pounding, thumping, bounding,
now Thelma's here and sounding
promising. "Barbara? Who me? No fear,
she's the one I just can't bear".

17. Twelve and a half.

Kissing Hester is alright,
I s'pose,
once I can
navigate her nose,
although,
I'd rather kick a ball about,
or cut some rashers with a stone.

'Cause now I've got
this rotten cold sore.

It's a bloomin' bore!

18. Thirteen.

Behind the Bike shed, Daphne and me
linger now it's half past three
and though she's younger, much, than me,
more advanced she seems to be.

'Kiss me' she says, and I am blushing
as into my face the hot blood is rushing.
And now she really puts the wind up me, with
'What about mothers and fathers, after tea?'

19. Palindromic

It was in the March
of thirty-three,
the third it was
when the thought struck me.
The date!
Three,
  three and
    thirty-three,
significant surely
this must be?
And I wondered,
what, and where I'd be,
when a similar thing
came round again?
The fours,
  fives,
    sixes,
      sevens
        and eights
would they for me
be significant dates?

And now that these answers
are revealed to me,
and nine,
  nine,
    ninety-nine
        is next to be,
I wonder,
shall I see
a palindrome,
in the next century?

My paternal Grandmother was a widow right from the time I
first knew her, and probably for the second time around.

Short in stature, she was not more than about five feet in
height, and even in my earliest memory I saw her as a very
old lady. So it came as something of a surprise when I came
home from the second world war in 1945 just after she had
died to find that her gravestone recorded her age at the
time of her death as only seventy four. That very old lady
I visited in the 1920's was in reality only in her fifties.

It was probably those long black dresses that had just a
suggestion of white lace peeping out on to her black laced
up boots, together with her grey/black hair she tied in a
tight bun at the back that made her look older. She always
wore black so perhaps she was in perpetual mourning for her
lost husband, maybe husbands in the plural, I don't know.
What I do know is that she was one very fierce lady indeed!

And she had very strict rules for my visits. One was that I
was never, ever to go upstairs to her bedroom, so that when
she herself went up the narrow ladder like stair to get
money for me for shopping, she would "shoo" me away with
`You are not to follow me up here mind, and get away from
those stairs, nosey little wretch that's what you are!'

Naturally that bedroom intrigued me. What could an old lady
have up there in her bedroom that she needed to guard so
jealously? Money perhaps? A miser's hoard hidden away
maybe? I never did get up there to see, try as I might.

20. Cat's Whisker Christmas.

Long, long ago, it seems,
almost as though it's in my dreams
as through my memory's mist
there gleams,
lingering, loving thoughts
and dearest fond esteem.

And as I stare this monitor screen,
backward, backward
goes the dream,
shutting out the years between,
forgetting torments, painful scenes,
forgetting too the happiness
and joy that there has been.

To open the paths of memory,
deep down in the brain
and live those happy childhood days
all over once again.

Sweep away the fog of time
and slowly, slowly,
it's refined,
those earliest images contained
are all that now remain.

And now I see it, clear,
quite plain,
a little boy
I'm six again,
in trousers short
and socks down,
running, skips the lane.

Past one, past two and three, to four,
this very last one is Granny's door
and its standing open
waiting for,
my late arrival
half past four.

Granny Emmence, so very old,
small and wrinkled
fierce and bold,
gives me a doctored sugar lump
and says that it will cure my cold.
`I haven't got one Granny!'
But she never will be told

and she's cross, because I'm late
and saying she simply cannot wait
this miracle to witness,
and quickly closes up the door,
puts the curtain straight.

Standing on the table
is a small square wooden box,
with a Speaker Horn
`His Master's Voice',
sitting on the top

and there is a battery, some wires
and three round knobs.
`It's a Cat's Whisker Wireless'
Grandma says to me,
but this I cannot understand,
for wires I plainly see!

And now she starts to fiddle
Granny's anxious I can see
as she says `It's very difficult,
to get the B.B.C.'

Noises hissing, rude abound
as Granny turns the knobs around
and puts her ear in close,
until some tuneful music
comes flooding all around
to fill the room with sound.

They sing that
Christ is born this day,
and then we hear them kneel to pray,
the Bishop give his Blessing
and they sing The Great Amen.

But Granny took so long
to tune the station in,
that nearly all the service
and the singing we have missed.
And though 'twas all her doing,
I know that she'll blame me

as she puts the cloth on
sets the tea
grumbling still
she glares at me.
`You come when I tell you,
or else you leave me be!'

But what a wondrous thing it is
I've shared with her today,
a Carol and the Blessing
the Bishop there to say.
And from St Martins in the Fields,
in London, all the way!

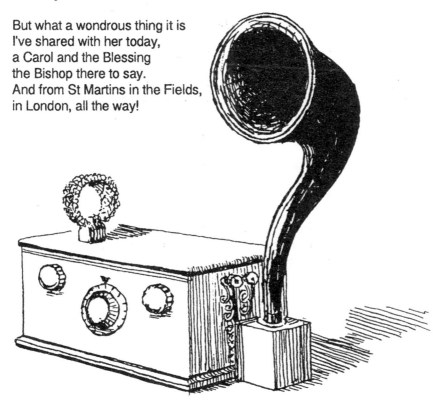

It was not until the mid 1930's that electricity, and therefore electric light, made much impression on the village of King's Somborne. I can be fairly sure of the timing because that is when my brother John, Jack to family, left school to work at Arthur Page's garage as an apprentice fitter and in doing so became involved in the first attempts to provide the village with electric light.

The other local garage also started up a similar scheme soon after so that rivalry then became intense. How the village came to have two garage businesses when hardly anyone could afford a car was something of a mystery. Even more of a mystery is the fact that now in the 1990's, when almost every local family owns two cars at least, we have only one part time garage with just one petrol pump!

Those first electrical experiments that had the wires strung around the village from tree to tree were inevitably Heath Robinson. For one thing, there was little or no back-up storage capacity so that customers only had power whilst the generators were working and often they were not, almost always breaking down just as it was getting dark.

The wires too got broken or tangled up in the trees by any wind above a breeze and this meant that my brother Jack was constantly turning out to make re-connections.

But eventually between them they did get a reasonably reliable service operating. Then the Grid came through the village and took away all their customers!

21. Mod. Cons c.1930's.

Smoking oil lamps guttering candles,
Hurricane lights with red hot handles,
Carbide lanterns smelly, hissing,
Tilley lamps flaring. Footsteps missing.

With electric light then all the rage,
Charlie Emmence and Arthur Page,
garage proprietors and business rivals,
both decided to install generators.

Then to show their confidence, in the innovation,
they wired up their houses, as a demonstration.
And so it was that Somborne, a long delay despite,
caught up with the world, switched on electric light.

But if all the lights were burning
at the beginning of the line,
the ones most distant from the source
just simply failed to shine.

Repairs were also difficult for when a wire broke,
you couldn't turn the power off and were
integrated in the system, conductor for the load.
So to make that re-connection, needed bravery untold.

Now-a-days of course, we're long since on the Grid,
white plastic switches, wires concealed all hid.
But even in the nineties, it hasn't come to pass,
no-one with the enterprise, to start up with the Gas!

I mentioned earlier some of the smells that invaded my
young nostrils and that have stayed on with me. Another of
these is smoke.

In a village with a great deal of thatch it is not
surprising that there were frequent house fires creating
smoke, my Mother lived in constant fear that ours would be
the next one.

22. Smell Smoke.

Many things seen and many things heard
sights once beheld or the spoken word,
are fleeting,
transient,
passing.
Gone.

But smells one never does forget
from earliest childhood remembered yet,
for ever they stay,
won't go away,
permanent.
Set.

Grandfather, whisker ends stained brown
from the chimney corner sitting down,
and wood fires at work,
`fug' at the Crown,
tobacco.
Smoke.

The Village Blacksmith, furnace flaring
hammers horse shoes, white hot, searing,
makes a fitting,
horny hoof,
acrid burning.
Smoke.

Guy Fawkes night and bonfires blazing
Roman Candles, Rockets raising
Oo's and Ah's and
crashing sounds.
Thunderflashes.
Smoke.

Not eyes nor ears that bring it back
for power to span the time they lack,
much more evocative
the nose is,
smelling.
Smoke.

Try to picture a huge inglenook fireplace with bench seats right up beside of the fire on each side and a sooty black kettle hanging from a chain in the chimney where bacon joints are also being smoked.

23. Chimney Corner.

Ask me where I'd like to be,
say anywhere in the world, feel free
and anything I'd ask for
you'd then arrange for me.

On a transatlantic liner in a best Stateroom,
on a spaceship mission, flying to the moon,
at a Frank Sinatra concert, just to sit and swoon
and listen to the magic of a Gershwin tune.

Cast out a fly upon the river Spey,
spend a night at a Casino making hay,
go with Captain Kirk to ride the milky way,
or in a football stadium watch the world teams play.

See the magic of a sunset on the river Nile,
the Pyramids, the Sphinx and stay a while.
Climb the Himalayas high, for miles and miles,
or shoot the Amazon rapids in the very best style.

Ask me again where would I like to be
and without hesitation my answer you would see.
In the chimney corner sit, dear Mum and me,
back in those happy childhood days,
of nineteen twenty-three.

24. A Child's Wind Quartet.

Westerly

When March winds blow westerly
and rip in from the Irish Sea,
fishermen make towards the lee
and sailboats racing landwards flee.
Tight the buds it shakes, unfurls,
in nooks and crannies, pokes and swirls,
O'r Ash and Elm, Rooks caw, dive, whirl,
as branches high, sway, bend and curl.
It pulls and buffets, tugs with glee
scattering winter's dead debris.
Round eaves and gutters, indignantly,
snug in my playroom, it howls at me.

Southerly

South winds of summer, gentler be
on gulf stream from the Arabian sea.
Rooks can build, glide gracefully
and quiet now the great Elm tree.
Bring sweet seducing showers of rain
to salve the parched earth's thirst and pain,
then, sweeping clear the skies again,
warm healing sunshine does obtain.
And soft it sings its voice caressing
from the warm earth, nature's blessing.
Sees me in the garden playing
and talks to me as gentle praying.

Northerly

But when there's talk of cold and snow
and experts forecast twelve below,
it's then north winds of winter blow
and tender shoots no longer grow.
South from Greenland's icy shores,
round the rafters, windows roars,
piercing cracks around the doors
penetrating panes and pores.
But on the hearth the log fire bright
and Christmas Tree. Heart warming sight.
Though cold the wind on Christmas night
it speaks to me of pure delight.

Easterly

Early springtime, sun and snow melt,
easterly, biting cold the wind felt,
o'er barren Fenlands, home of the Celt,
dry the earth, hard caked the veldt.
Field Mouse, Vole, hibernate, hide,
Fox must forage far and wide
prowling the Hen House, dinner inside,
penned for the night all safe abide.
Weathermen gloomy, warn beware,
chill factor twenty we should fear
but Snowdrop and Crocus buds appear,
as the east wind's voice I hear.

But what a mixed up sound there'd be
a howl, sigh, moan, roar, symphony.
Weathercock wildly spin would he,
if all four winds at once blew free.

Between the two great wars, Arthur Smith was an important village employer with his Steam Threshing business. These next two sets of verses are intended as a tribute to the few survivors who did this kind of work. Steam for many of them became a way of life right up to the end.

Charlie Reeves was one such and his father, who was also a fine tenor voice in the church choir, is the engine driver in "Steam Threshing". I am the lad 'late for work again'.

Charlie was at least the third generation of Reeves' to carry on this family tradition and he remained a steam enthusiast right up to the time of his death, owning his own engine and attending all the major Steam Rallies. He featured with his engine in a television programme just months before he died.

25. Steam Threshing c.1936.

Early morning, frosty, cold,
hardly light and Cock not crowed.
`Come on lad, you're late again,
work time going down the drain'.

Father did this work before, now dead,
dust got on his chest, Mum said.
And the work is dusty, hard,
once we leave the tackle yard.

Stoke the engine, check the tackle
put some grease upon the shackle.
Threshing, baling through the day,
dark before we've earned our pay.

`Fire burns hot lad, make some tea,
strong and sweet, two spoons for me'

Up on the footplate, Woodbines out,
offers the packet. `Have a drag',
twists a spill and lights the fag,
quoffs the tea, enjoys the "drag".

Heave the throttle lever round
to fill the day with a powerful sound,
the funnel belching smoke and sparks.
`Watch the gate lad'. Journey starts.

Four full ricks to thrash today
before the Tackle pulls away,
oil lamps burning, arms, legs, tired,
home to the tackle yard, pull the fire.

26. Goodbye Charlie.

To a steam enthusiast.

Lies cold the hand that turned the lathe,
lies silent too the Anvil's ring
as belts, that once life's rhythm hummed
hang sagging, slack and still,
and never shall see the flywheel spin.

By Foden, Fowler, Watson and Haig,
at Stourpaine, Landford and Netley Marsh,
firebox glowing, hot, and stoking...
smoke and steam by snorting stack...
and throbbing, thrusting pistons, hissing...

...as steam at Blandford Forum is feted
sounds and smells fill the Dorset air.
`Has anybody seen Charlie Reeves?'
`Oh, haven't Ee heard the news my dear?
Old Charlie? Why, Ee be dead, last year!'

27. `Ow was Ee?'

The scoreboard on the pavilion wall,
tells it all.
Nine batsmen already heard the call.
One more, that's all.

Total for the visitors score,
so far a meager forty-four
last man none, not a single run.
One lonely spectator enjoying the fun.

Forty-nine, the home sides score
doesn't add up to a miser's hoard,
so just one more, and then a four
to equal this home side's miserable score.

Give them a cheer! Whatever for?

The Wicket keeper comes up close,
a stumping or an edge, he hopes.
Whilst Silly Mid-On
at the wicket edge
a popped up catch
he hopes to snatch
or at any rate
to intimidate
the tail end batsman
make him nervous
he's impervious,
never played the game before.

Watch out now for the leg before!

And now the left arm bowler, slow,
prepares to deliver the final blow,
starts his run up,
one, two, three
gives it a tweak
and sets it free,
plenty of air
tantalizing
hanging there
hits the ground
with one bound,
bounces up and strikes the pad.

`How's that!' the yell
'twas wide as ---- well,
Dicky Shorter gives him out
points his finger to the sky.
A delighted shout
from fielders
rings about
they're all out,
there is no more.

What a bore!

28. Cemetery.

Life's ending brought much pain and care,
and when we buried Mother here
it worried me, that she should be,
left in this cold, deep, dark scree.

But time heals all, and now I see
that when she passed to eternity,
there was no need for misery
for in God's care, safe, warm she'll be.

29. Second Childhood.

Lucas Greenwood is my best friend,
    our play together should never end.
Buggy brmm, brmm the pavements wend,
    for ever the land of let's pretend.

And Lucas takes me to the park,
    homeward when it's almost dark.
Ride on the piggywig, what a lark
    and did you hear that doggie bark?

Bang the drum and blow the band,
    with instruments in every hand.
Read my book please, Postman Pat, and,
    content as any in the land.

Long days of play so much to do,
    fun and frolic the whole day through.
Which the infant? Tell me do,
    one past seventy, the other two!